the first living things

the first

illustrated by howard berelson

Text copyright © 1970 by Julian May Dikty. Illustrations copyright © 1970 by Holiday House, Inc.

First published in Great Britain 1972 by Blackie & Son Limited,
5 Fitzhardinge Street, London WIH ODL
Bishopbriggs, Glasgow G64 2NZ.

Printed in Great Britain by R. & R. Clark, Ltd., Edinburgh

ISBN 0 216 89524 3.

julian may

Living things

Blackie: London and Glasgow

Once, billions of years ago, there were
two worlds going around the sun together.
The larger world was our planet, the earth.
The smaller one was the moon.
Neither world had any living things.

Both the earth and the moon were hot.
They were not solid, but liquid. Around
both of the worlds swirled clouds of gas,
called atmospheres.

As time went by, the worlds began to cool off.
Hard crusts formed on their outsides.
But they were still hot inside, and volcanoes
threw up gases and liquid rock. The moon
and earth were covered with dust and ashes.

The moon was small, and so the downward pull of its
gravity was weak. Little by little the gases
of its atmosphere leaked away into space.
Now and then a volcano would throw out more gas,
but it soon escaped from the moon. The little
world could not keep an atmosphere.

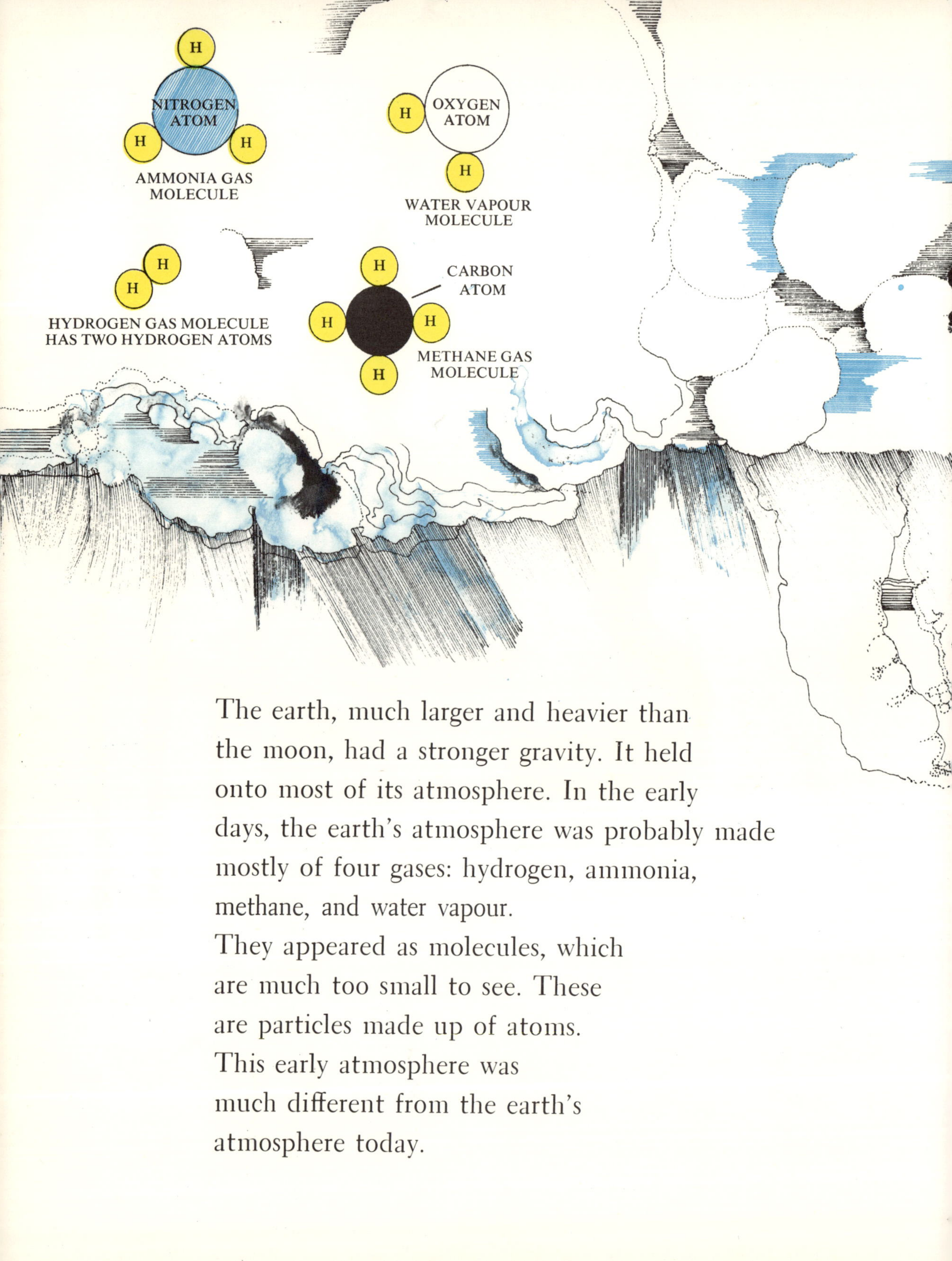

The earth, much larger and heavier than the moon, had a stronger gravity. It held onto most of its atmosphere. In the early days, the earth's atmosphere was probably made mostly of four gases: hydrogen, ammonia, methane, and water vapour.

They appeared as molecules, which are much too small to see. These are particles made up of atoms. This early atmosphere was much different from the earth's atmosphere today.

The water vapour cooled and turned to rain.
When the rain first fell on the hot earth's
crust, the water turned to vapour again.
The vapour rose upward, cooled and formed
clouds—and then rain fell once more.

It rained for millions and millions of years.
When the crust grew cooler, the rain began to
form small oceans.

But on the moon, all was still. There
was no atmosphere and no water. Lightning
flashed over the clouded earth, but the
moon had only the glow of a volcano from time
to time.

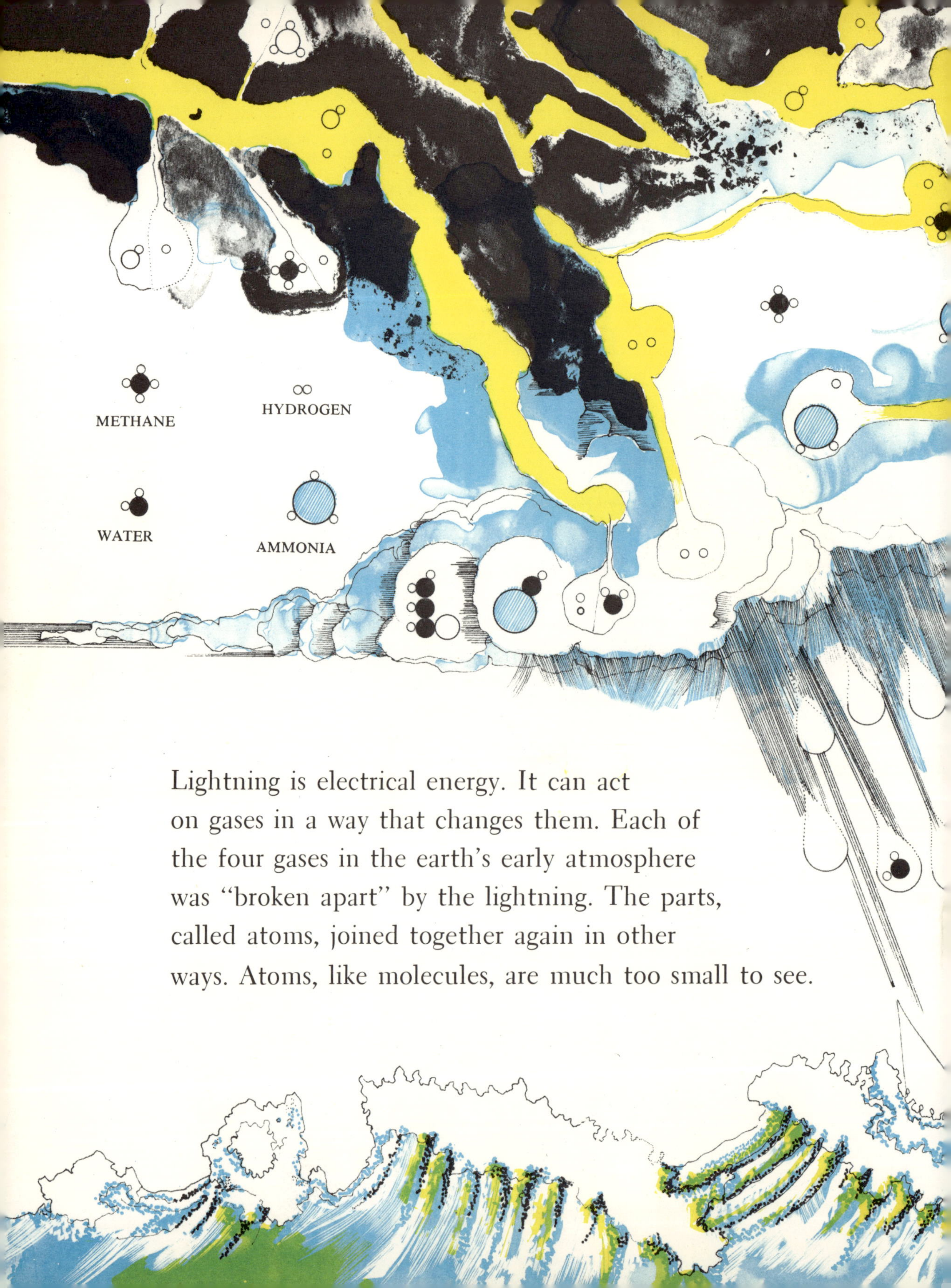

Lightning is electrical energy. It can act
on gases in a way that changes them. Each of
the four gases in the earth's early atmosphere
was "broken apart" by the lightning. The parts,
called atoms, joined together again in other
ways. Atoms, like molecules, are much too small to see.

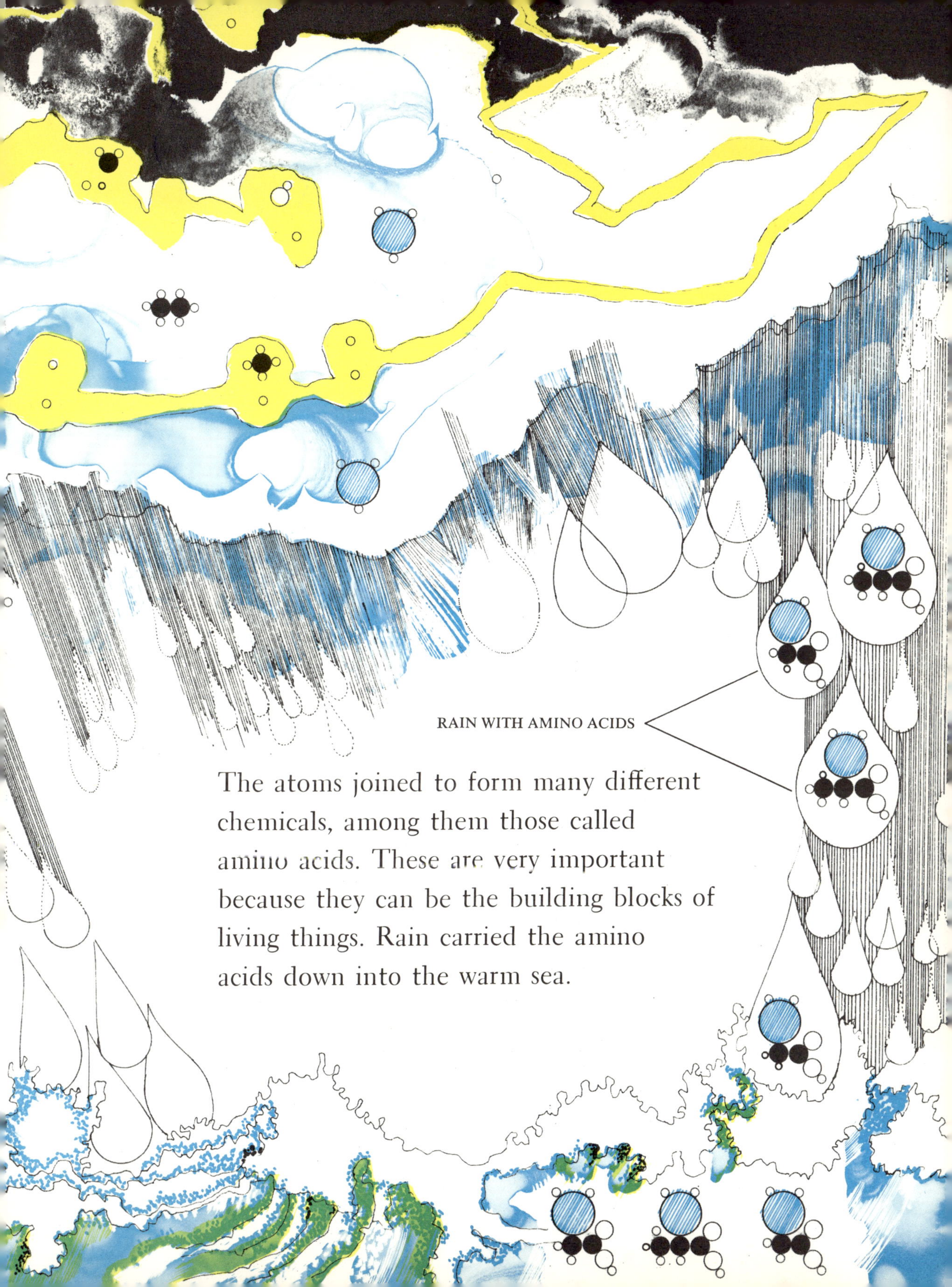

The atoms joined to form many different chemicals, among them those called amino acids. These are very important because they can be the building blocks of living things. Rain carried the amino acids down into the warm sea.

More and more amino acids formed. After
millions of years the sea was an amino-acid
"soup." The lightning storms came less often; but the
sun's rays were also helping to make amino
acids in the atmosphere. Some of the soup
was thrown onto the hot, dry land. As the
soup dried, amino acids were able to join
together to form chains.

Later, when it rained again, the chains
were washed back into the sea. This could
have happened over and over again, with the
chains getting longer each time. Chains
might also have been growing in the sea.
Amino acids linked into long chains are
called protein molecules. They are much
bigger than atoms, but still too small to see.

Protein molecules are not living things.
But they are the stuff from which all living
things are made. As more proteins formed,
the molecules bumped into each other and
sometimes stuck together. Tiny droplets
of protein matter formed.

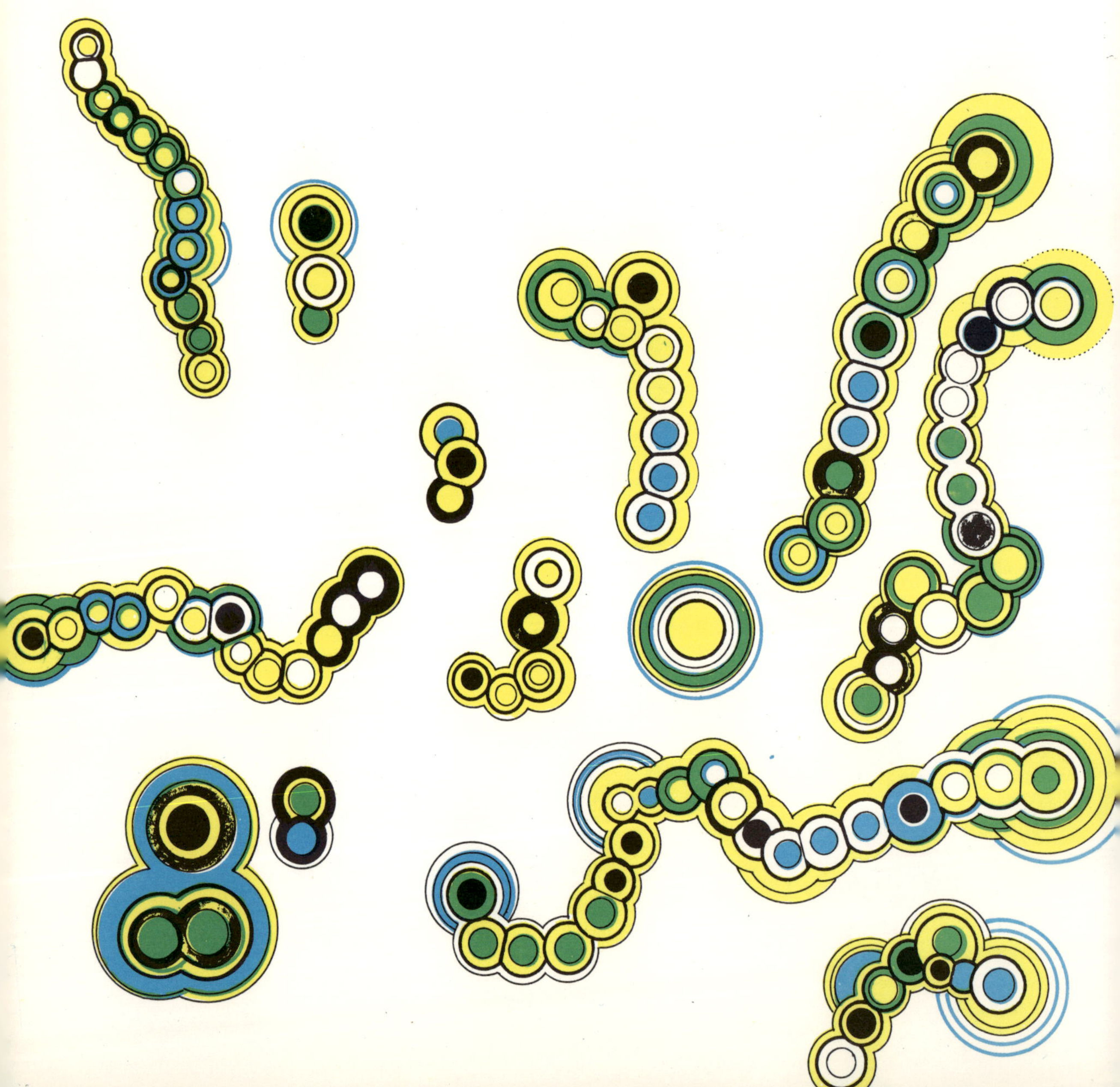

The droplets gathered together into larger
masses that we can call "blobs." Some blobs
were able to get energy from the soup around
them. They "discovered" how to take in soup-
chemicals and change them into energy or into
still larger molecules.

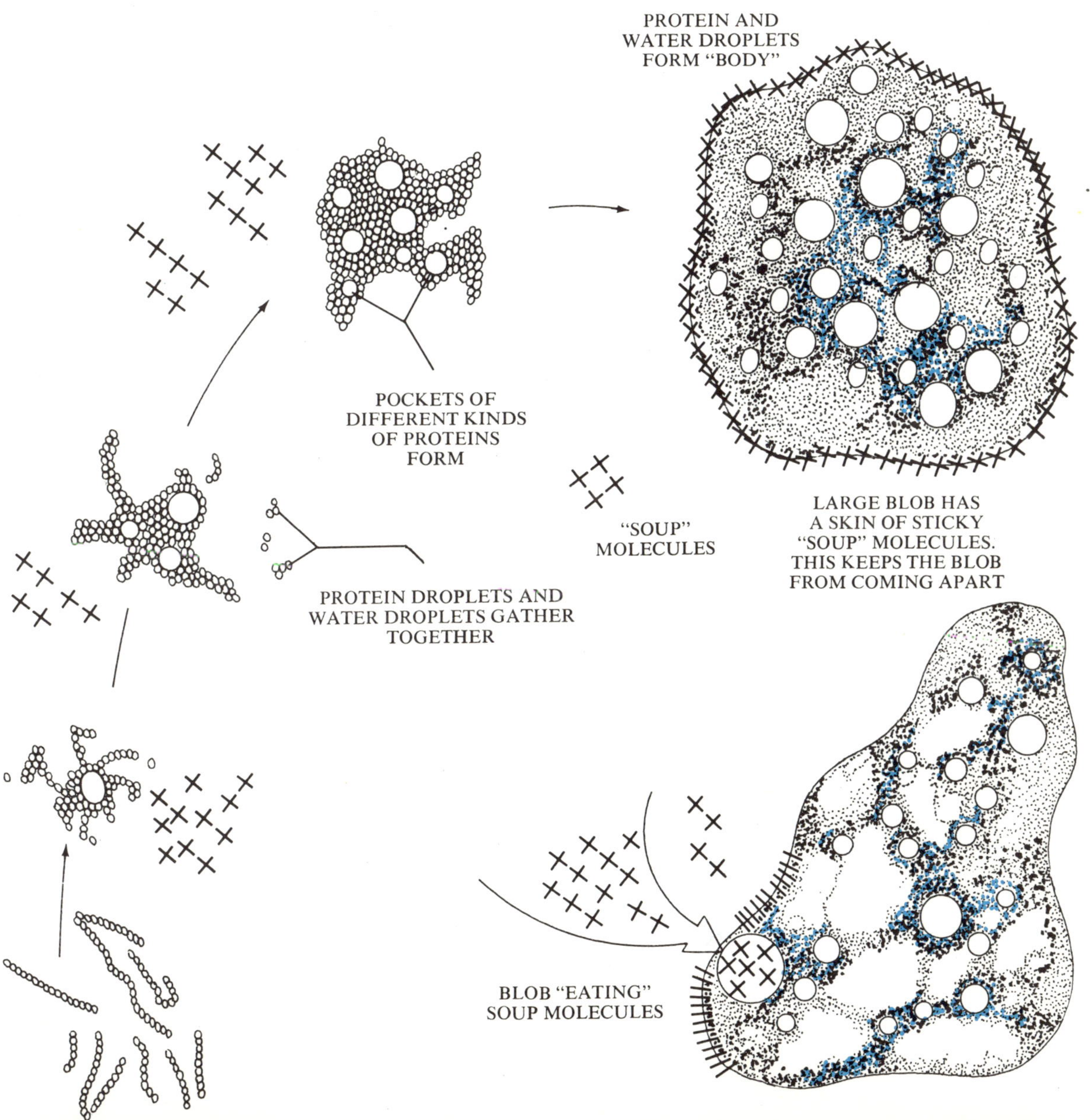

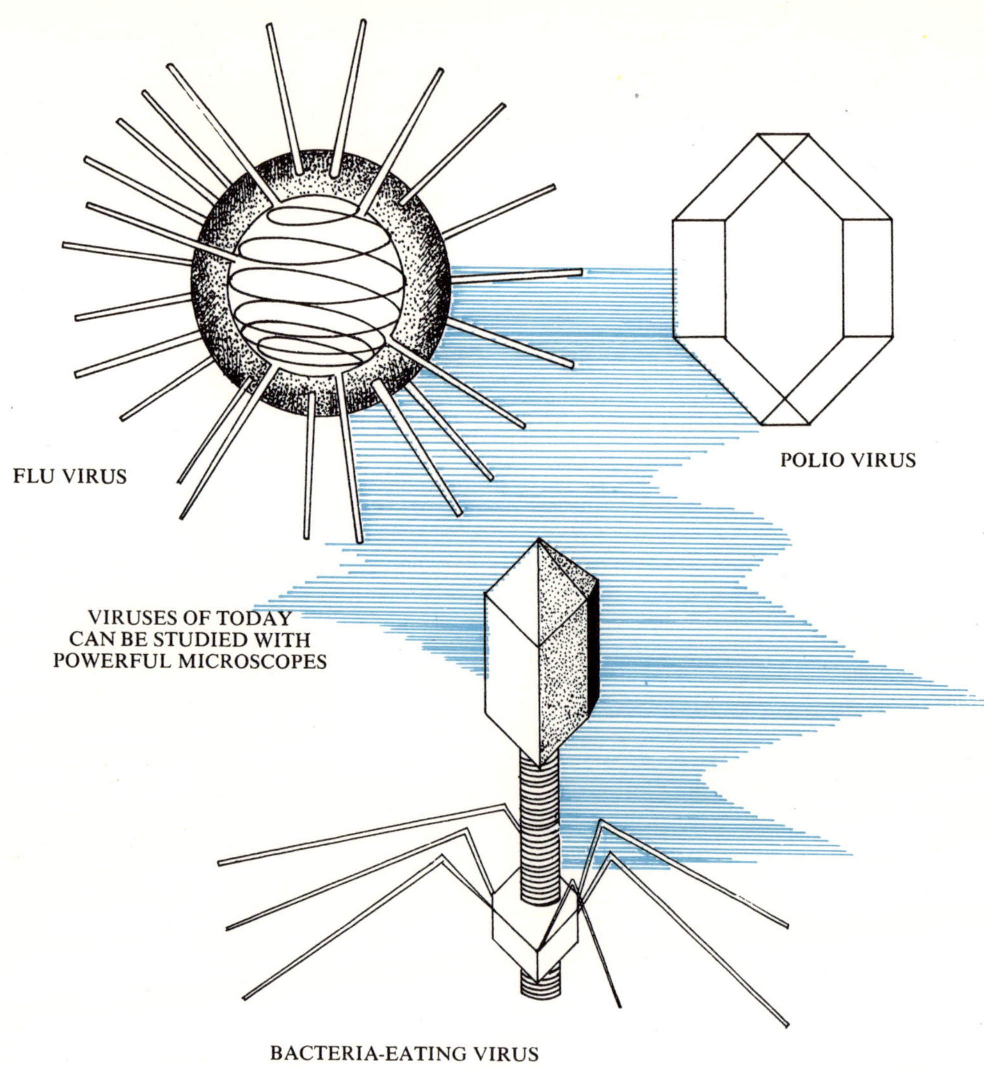

Were the protein blobs the first living things? It is not easy to say. Some very simple living things, such as today's viruses, act something like living things and something like non-living chemicals. Maybe the blobs did too.

Some kinds of blobs probably did not last
long. They broke apart into amino acids
again. Other blobs were more of a success.
When they grew large, they broke into pieces
that could keep on growing. These blobs
could reproduce, or make others like themselves.

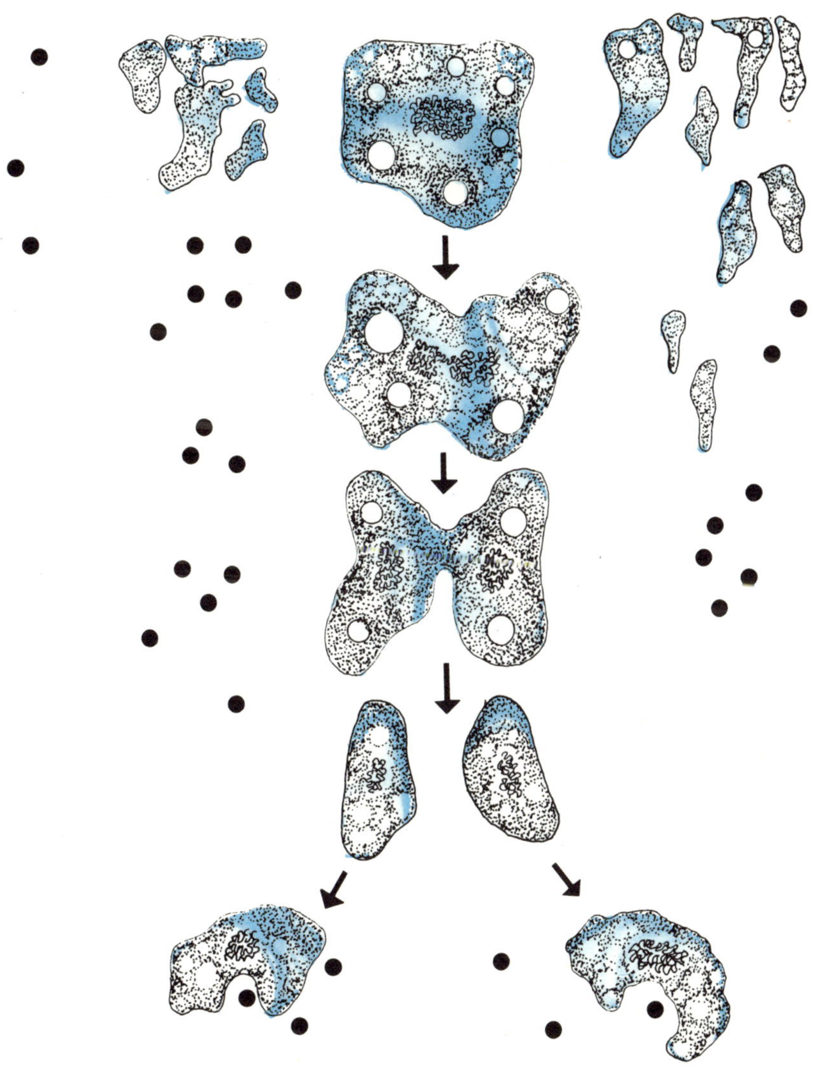

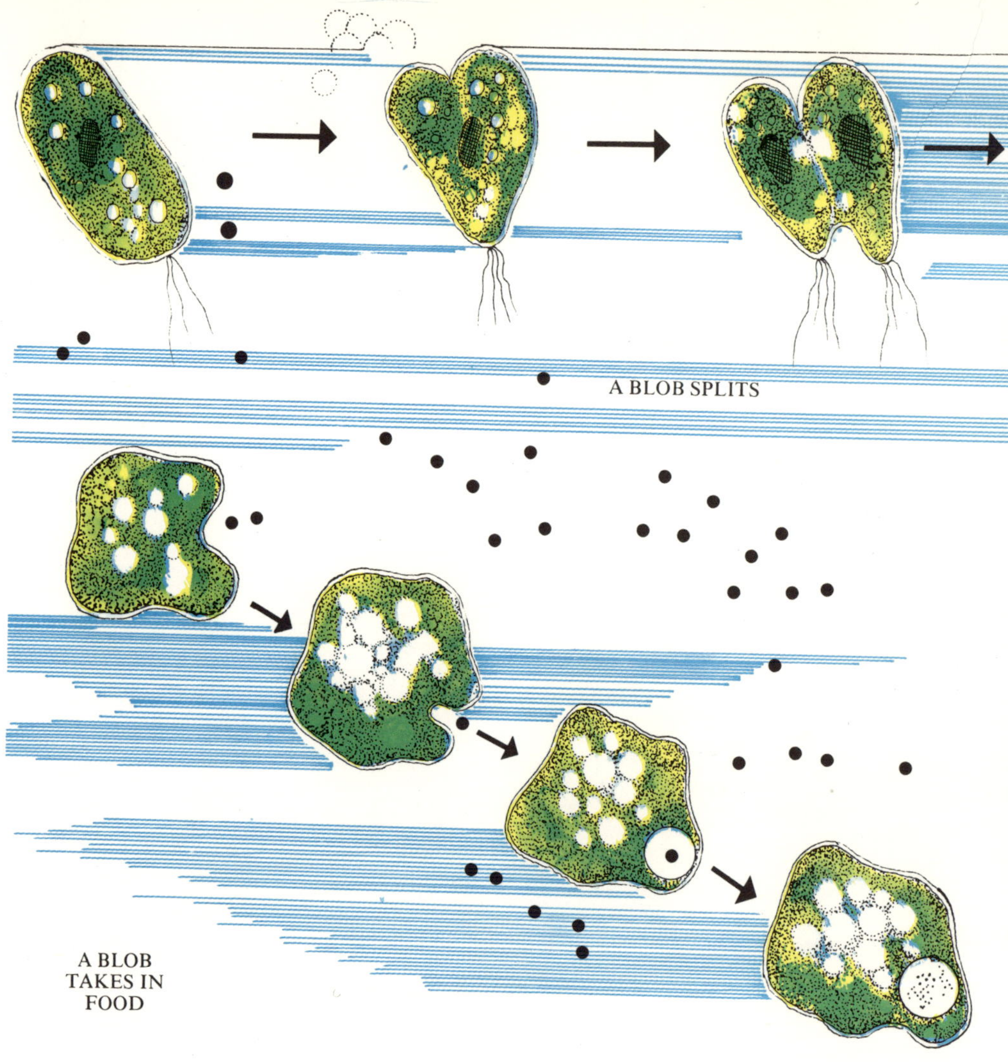

The most successful blobs must have slowly
changed into the first real living things.
We can call these things the "food-eaters,"
because they "ate" the soup-chemicals in
the warm sea of long ago.

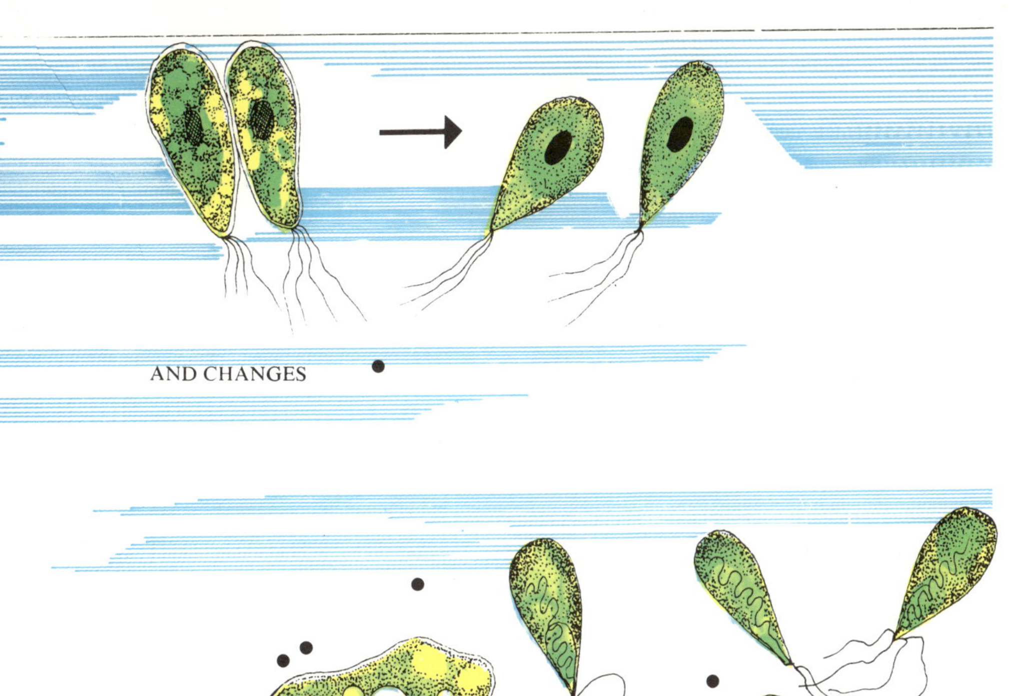

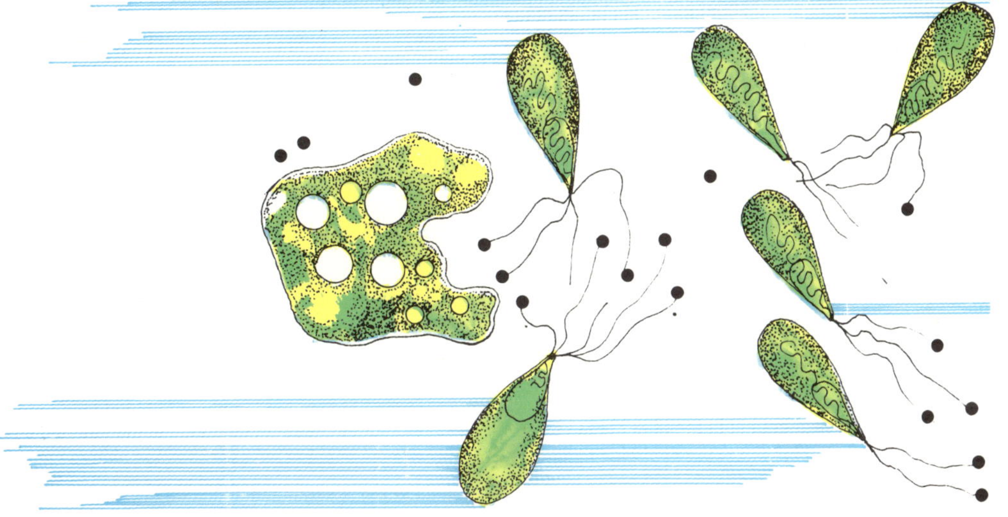

When food-eaters reproduced, they usually
made new living things just like the old ones.
But once in a while changes occurred. A food-
eater would split and produce new ones that
were different. If the new ones could make
better use of the food, they grew and reproduced
faster than the old food-eaters.

The slow changing of living things into new forms is called evolution. Many kinds of simple food-eaters must have evolved in the early days of the earth. All of them were very tiny and all lived in the sea. On the dry moon there were no living things at all because life must have water.

No one knows very well what the earliest living things
looked like. They have left rather uncertain fossils, or
traces in the rocks. They may have looked
something like the things shown in the picture.

Time passed, and the food-eaters used up much
of the amino-acid soup. It was getting harder
to make a living by taking in food from outside
the body. One day a new living thing appeared.
It not only ate soup, but it could also take
energy from the sun's rays and make food right
inside its own body.

SOME LIVING THINGS
COULD MAKE FOOD WITH
THE HELP OF SUNLIGHT

The first food-makers used sunlight to put
together water and a gas, carbon dioxide.
They made sugars and starches, which are food.
These living things could use the food to
make new living matter, or they could change
the food into energy.

WHEN THERE WAS NO SUNLIGHT,
THEY COULD EAT "SOUP"

The food-makers evolved into the first plants.
The means they used for making food is called
photosynthesis. As the plants made food, they
also gave off oxygen. This gas passed into the
earth's atmosphere.

TODAY'S ONE-CELLED ALGAE,
WHICH ARE MOSTLY WATER PLANTS,
ARE SOMETHING LIKE THE
FIRST PLANTS OF LONG AGO

The living things that used photosynthesis
best were green plants. They reproduced very
quickly and filled the seas. They made large
amounts of oxygen and changed the earth's atmosphere.
The oxygen that we breathe today was made
mostly by green plants.

Food-eaters still lived. But now, instead
of feeding upon amino-acid soup, they began
to feed upon the food-making plants. These
plant-eaters were the first animals. They
not only ate plants, but they also used
oxygen from the atmosphere. This oxygen
released energy from the plant-food.

The plants and animals helped each other
to live. As the animals used food, they
gave off carbon dioxide gas. This was taken
in by the green plants and used to make
more food. As plants and animals died, their
bodies broke down into many kinds of chemicals
and became a kind of fertilizer for the plants.

Evolution continued. New kinds of plants
and animals appeared on the earth. They began
to live on land as well as in the sea. New
living things kept evolving for million of years.

We can see traces of many early living
things as fossils in rocks. But the
fossils are really clear only for the
last 600 million years or so. We know life
is much older than this—probably more
than three billion years old.

The first living things are gone without
a trace. But scientists can study the
ways these things might have formed and
grew. An artificial atmosphere, like that
of the early earth, can be placed in a container.

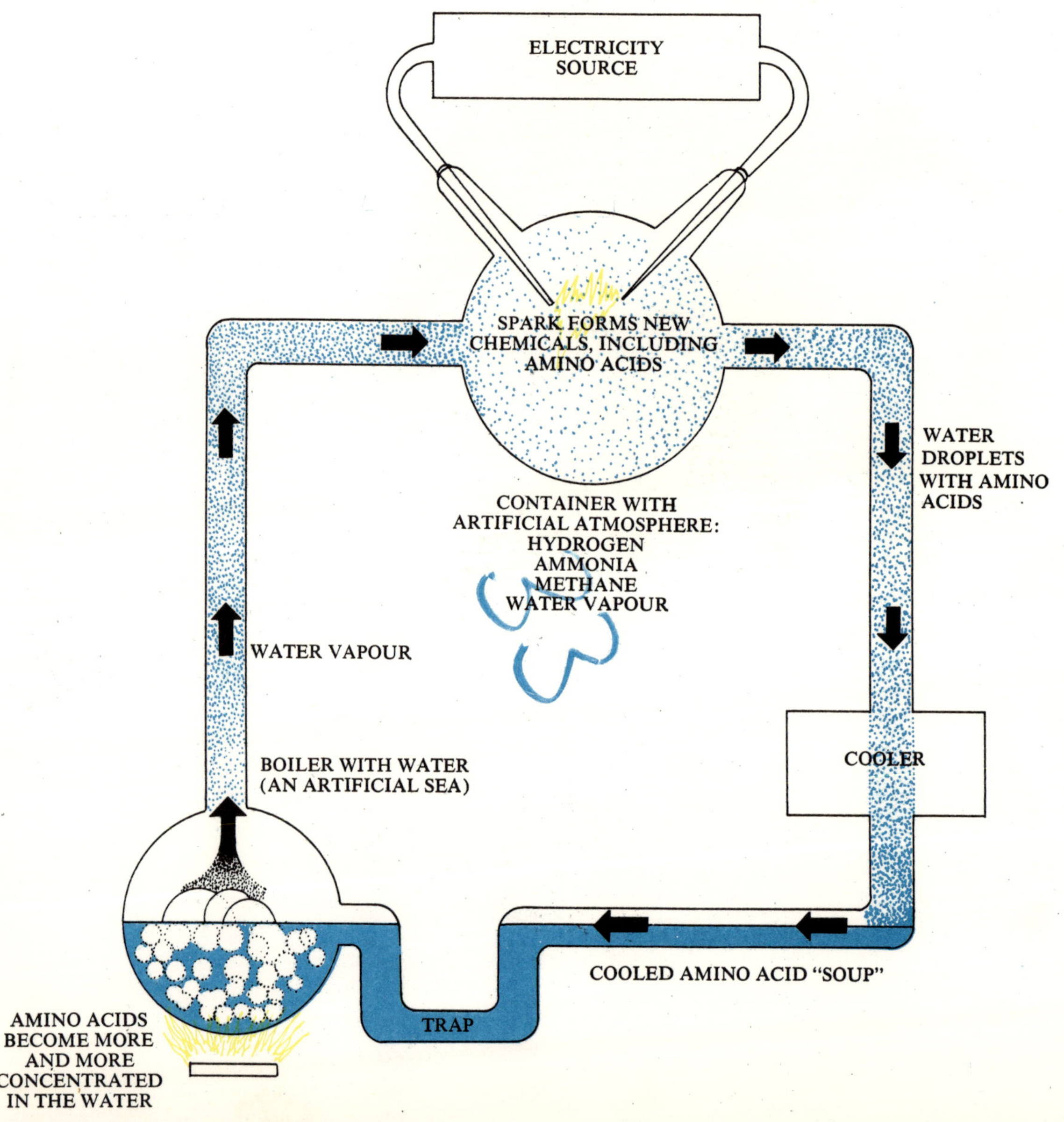

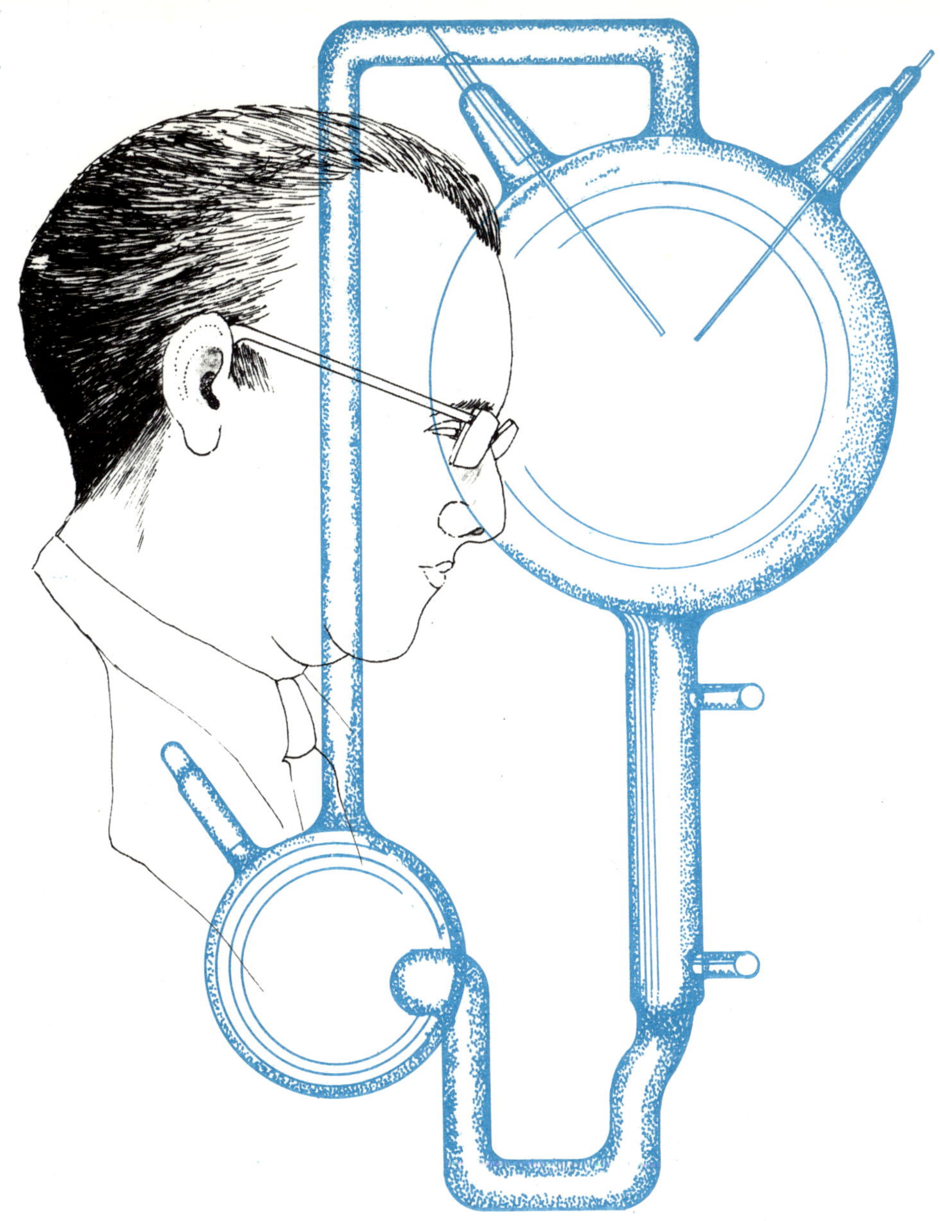

Electric sparks can take the place of the
early lightning. A scientist named Stanley
Miller made amino acids from the gases hydrogen,
ammonia, methane, and water vapour by sending
sparks through them again and again.

Today the earth contains many forms of life.
But most scientists think that new life no
longer forms naturally from non-living chemicals
as it did in the beginning. The atmosphere has
changed. It is no longer full of ammonia,
methane, and hydrogen. Now the earth's atmosphere
is mostly nitrogen, oxygen, and carbon dioxide.
Lightning and sunlight cannot make amino acids
from these gases.

Today, new life seems to come only from older life. Plants produce new plants, and animals have young. No more swarms of protein blobs live in the sea. But someday scientists may be able to make them so we can study them.

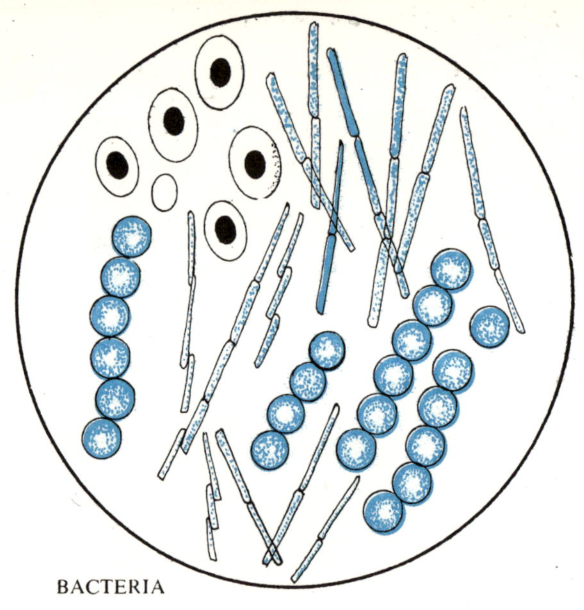

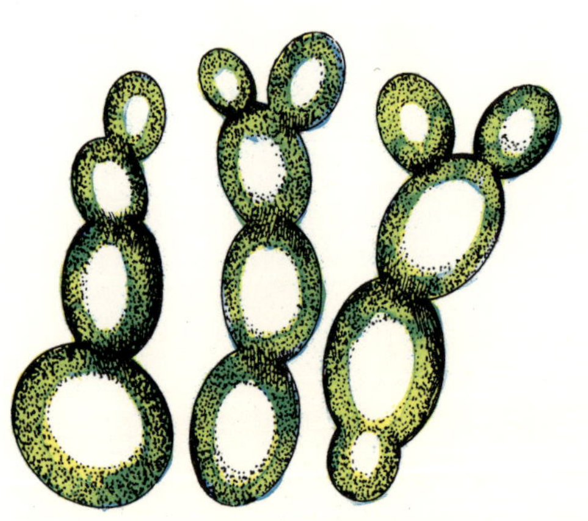

Some kinds of simple food-eating plants
remain on the earth. They are bacteria, yeasts,
fungi, and other plants that are not green.
They do not live on amino-acid soup; it is
gone from the sea. Instead, they take
chemicals from the soil and from many other
places—including the bodies of men and animals.

Thousands and thousands of different green
plants live today. They are food-makers for
themselves, for animals, and for mankind.
And food-making plants continue to make the
oxygen we need to breathe.

More thousands of animals live on earth today. Some eat plants; some eat other animals; some eat both plants and animals. All animals are food-eaters, but they are quite different from the first food-eating living things.

Today, two worlds still move around the sun
together. The moon is cold, dry, all but
airless, and without life. The earth is
warm and green, covered with oceans and
wrapped in a moist atmosphere full of oxygen.
Our planet is beautiful and alive.

author's note

No one knows the exact nature of the atmosphere of the primeval earth, and it is also impossible to state with certainty just how the first living things arose. This book presents some widely accepted theories in a simplified form. The protein systems termed "blobs" are coacervates. The "food-eaters" are primitive heterotrophs; the "food-makers" are autotrophs.